Super Focus

Unleashing Your Productivity Potential

Avtar Garcha

Contents

FOCUS

Introduction

Staying focused can be tough in the modern world with constant stream of distractions these days i.e., social media, emails, phone calls to name a few.

You must understand your brain's limitations with all the noise around and still works around it to increase your focus and productivity.

Do one thing at a time and do it well. Do not try! to be a Superhero. It only happens in the movies.

Reality is different. Be real. Do not try to multitask. Focus on the job at hand and give it! your hundred percent. Success will be yours. Focus helps you to avoid distracting. thoughts, improve your concentration and enable you to act more efficiently.

Focus is the ability to direct one's attention by one is will. It is the ability to keep the mind targeted at the subject without any distraction.

Our mind is constantly at work whether we are aware or unaware of the process. Every act needs focus to bring it to fruition.

Whether you are studying, working, playing or conversing or even washing utensils, etc. need focus.

The bad focus will make you a bad listener and you will miss what is happening around. you and you may miss some good opportunities in life.

If you are doing one thing and thinking about something else, it means you are not present in the moment. Your mind is wandering elsewhere while you are physically present here.

Remember focus can lead you to success in any and every field of your life. Few things like meditation, good sleep, keeping distractions like phones, social media etc. away can also help you in decluttering your brain and help in increasing focus.

David Rock, Co-founder of The Neuro Leadership Institute and author of "Your Brain At Work" (Harper Collins 2009) says," Distractions signal that something has changed"." A distraction is an alert that says, Orient your attention here now and that could! be dangerous."

"Twenty minutes of deep focus could be. transformative," Rock says, Your goal is not constant focus but a short distraction-free time every day.

You can try the following three steps to help. you become more focused and productive.

1. Do creative work first Our brains are wired to do mindless work first and leave the toughest tasks to the last.

That drains our energy and lowers our focus." An hour into doing your work, you have a lot less capacity than at the beginning" Rock! speaks.

Every decision we make tires the brain. You.

2.Must reverse the order to focus effectively.

Check off the tasks that require concentration or creativity first thing in the morning and then move on to easier tasks like checking your mail, social media, etc. for later.

2 Allocate your time deliberately.

Rock studied thousands of people and found. that we are truly focused for an average of only six hours per week. "You want to be. diligent with what you put into the hours," he speaks. Most people focus early in the morning or late. t night. Rock's study shows that 90% of the people do their best thinking away from them. usual place of work. But there are no hard and fast rules about it.

You must work out when and where. you focus best and then allocate your toughest tasks for those moments.

3.Train your mind like a muscle

Rock says," We have trained our brains to be. unfocussed" Your brain quickly adapts when. you are multi-tasking. Practice concentration! by turning off the distractions and focusing all your attention to the task at hand.

Start small. Remember somebody asked this question." How do you eat an elephant?"

The answer was "Bite by bite" Start focusing! five minutes a day and work it up to larger. chunks of time.

If you find your mind wandering, just return to the task at hand. Rock says, "It is just like getting fit. You must build the muscle to be focused."

It is difficult to stay mentally focused when you are worrying about the future or reliving the past. or just distracted out of the present moment for some other reason.

It is all about putting away distractions whether. they are psychological (your anxieties) or of the physical kind (your mobile phone, laptop etc.)

To keep your focus in the moment you must stay engaged and keep your attention sharp.

It might take some time but keep on learning to truly live in the moment.

Mastering Focus
1.Understanding Focus

Now we delve into the concept of focus. We explore what focus is, its significance, and how it impacts various aspects of our lives.

Focus is the ability to direct our attention and energy towards a specific task or goal while ignoring distractions.

We discuss the several types of focus, such as sustained focus, selective focus, and divided focus and how they manifest in our daily lives.

Focus is the concentrated attention on a specific task, concept, or goal, while ignoring distractions and irrelevant information.

It is the mental energy that directs our cognitive resources towards a singular objective. But focus is not merely about blocking out distractions; it is also about allocating your mental bandwidth efficiently.

In an age where distractions lurk around every corner, mastering the art of focus is akin to wielding a superpower.

Whether you are striving to complete a project, deepen your relationships, or pursue personal growth,

Types of Focus
1.Selective Focus

This involves concentrating on a particular stimulus. while filtering out other stimuli. For example, reading a book in a noisy café requires selective focus to drown. out the surrounding chatter.

2.Sustained Focus:

Sustaining attention over an extended period is

essential for tasks that demand prolonged mental engagement, such as studying for exams or drafting a thesis.

3.Divided Focus

Sometimes, we must divide our attention among multiple tasks simultaneously. However, dividing focus too thinly can reduce overall efficiency and quality of work.

The Importance of Focus
1.Productivity and Achievement

Focus is the cornerstone of productivity and achievement. When we are focused, we enter a state of flow, where time seems to slip away, and we perform at our peak. It allows us to complete tasks with greater efficiency and accuracy.

2.Creativity and Innovation

Contrary to the belief that focus stifles creativity, it fuels it. By immersing ourselves deeply in a problem or idea, we can uncover novel solutions and innovative insights.

3.Emotional Well-being

Focus can also enhance emotional well-being by reducing stress and anxiety. When we are absorbed in a task, our worries fade into the background, leading to a sense of calm and content.

CHAPTER 1

Cultivating Focus

1.Environment

Create an environment conducive to focus by minimizing distractions. This might involve finding a quiet workspace, turning off notifications, or using tools like noise-canceling headphones.

2.Time Management

Break your tasks into smaller, manageable chunks and allocate dedicated time slots for focused work. Use techniques like the Pomodoro Technique, where you work for a set period (e.g., 25 minutes) followed by a short break.

3.Mindfulness

Practice mindfulness to train your attentional muscles. Techniques like meditation can help improve focus by teaching you to observe your thoughts without judgment and redirect your attention when it wanders.

4.Prioritization

Identify your Most Important Tasks (MITs) and prioritize them. By focusing on high-value activities, you can make noteworthy progress towards your goals without getting bogged down by trivial matters.

5.Physical Health

Maintain a healthy lifestyle to support cognitive function. Regular exercise, proper nutrition, and adequate sleep are essential for optimizing focus and concentration.

Overcoming Challenges

1.Information Overload

In today's digital age, we are bombarded with information from all directions. To combat information overload, practice digital detox, social media, and curate your information diet consciously.

2.Multitasking

While multitasking may seem like a shortcut to productivity, it often leads to decreased efficiency and increased errors. Instead, focus on one task at a time, giving it your undivided attention before moving on to the next.

3.Procrastination

Procrastination is the antithesis of focus, tempting us to do unimportant tasks in favor of immediate gratification.

Combat procrastination by breaking tasks into smaller steps, setting deadlines and eliminating distractions.

Conclusion

In a world filled with distractions, focus is a rare and precious commodity. By understanding the nature of focus, recognizing its importance, and implementing strategies to cultivate and sustain it, you can unlock. your full potential and achieve greater success in every aspect of life.

CHAPTER 2

Factors Affecting Focus

Numerous internal and external factors can influence our ability to focus. In this chapter, we identify common factors that impact focus including sleep quality, stress levels, environmental distractions, and mental health conditions like anxiety and attention deficit hyperactivity disorder (ADHD). By recognizing these factors, we can take proactive steps to mitigate their effects and enhance our focus.

Focus, that elusive state of undivided attention, is influenced by a myriad of factors, ranging from external stimuli to internal states of mind. Understanding these factors is essential for optimizing focus and harnessing its power in our daily lives. In this chapter, we will explore the diverse array of elements that can either enhance or detract from our ability to concentrate.

External Factors
1.Environment

The physical environment plays a significant role in shaping our ability to focus. A cluttered workspace, noisy surroundings or uncomfortable seating can all create distractions and impede concentration. Conversely, a quiet, well-lit space with minimal disruptions can foster a conducive atmosphere for focused work.

2.Technology

While technology offers unparalleled opportunities for productivity and connectivity, it also poses significant challenges to focus. Constant notifications, social media feeds, and the allure of endless online content can hijack our attention and pull us away from important tasks. Setting boundaries around technology usage and implementing digital detoxes can help mitigate these distractions.

3.Social Interactions

Interactions with others can either bolster or undermine our focus, depending on the context. Collaborative work environments may enhance focus through shared goals and mutual accountability, while excessive socializing or interruptions can disrupt concentration. Establishing clear boundaries and communication norms can promote a balance between social interaction and focused work.

Internal Factors
1.Mental State

Our mental state profoundly influences our ability to focus. Stress, anxiety, and fatigue can impair concentration, making it difficult to sustain attention on tasks. Conversely, feelings of calmness, confidence, and motivation can enhance focus and cognitive performance. Practices such as mindfulness meditation, exercise, and adequate rest can help cultivate a positive mental state conducive to focus.

2.Emotional Regulation

Emotions play a pivotal role in shaping our focus. Strong emotions, such as excitement or frustration, can hijack our attention and impede cognitive control. Learning to regulate emotions through techniques like cognitive reappraisal, deep breathing, and progressive muscle relaxation can enhance our ability to maintain focus in the face of emotional challenges.

3.Physical Well-being

Physical health is closely intertwined with cognitive function and focus. Factors such as nutrition, hydration, and sleep quality can significantly impact our ability to concentrate. Maintaining a balanced diet, staying hydrated, and prioritizing restful sleep are essential components of a healthy lifestyle that supports optimal focus.

Cognitive Factors
1.Task Characteristics

The nature of the task itself influences our ability to focus. Tasks that are inherently engaging, challenging, and meaningful are more likely to capture our attention and sustain our interest. Breaking complex tasks into smaller, manageable components and setting clear goals can also enhance focus by providing a sense of direction and progress.

2.Cognitive Load

Cognitive load refers to the amount of mental effort required to perform a task. Tasks with high cognitive load, such as learning the latest information or solving complex problems, can tax our cognitive resources and make it challenging to maintain focus. Minimizing distractions, chunking information, and practicing selective attention can help manage cognitive load and improve focus.\\\\\\\\\

Conclusion

Focus is a multifaceted phenomenon shaped by a complex interplay of external and internal and cognitive factors.

By understanding these factors and their influence on our ability to concentrate, we can cultivate environments, mindsets, and habits that support optimal focus.

Whether it is creating a distraction-free workspace, managing stress and emotions, or adopting strategies to minimize cognitive load, mastering the factors influencing focus empowers us to unlock our full cognitive potential and achieve greater success in our endeavors.

CHAPTER 3

Techniques for Improving Focus

This chapter explores practical strategies and techniques for improving focus. In a world inundated with distractions, honing the ability to focus is a skill that can significantly enhance productivity, creativity, and overall well-being. Fortunately, there are numerous techniques and strategies that can help sharpen your focus and sustain attention on the task at hand. In this chapter, we will explore a variety of proven techniques for improving focus and boosting cognitive performance.

1. Pomodoro Technique

The Pomodoro Technique is a time management method that involves breaking work into intervals, typically 25 minutes in duration, separated by short breaks. This structured approach helps maintain focus by providing regular breaks to recharge and refocus attention.

2. Deep Work

Deep work refers to immersive, uninterrupted periods of concentrated focus on cognitively demanding tasks. Setting aside dedicated time for deep work, free from distractions and interruptions, allows for sustained attention and high-quality output.

3. Set Clear Goals

Establishing clear, achievable goals provides direction and motivation, making it easier to maintain focus on tasks. Break down larger goals into smaller, actionable steps, and prioritize tasks based on their importance and urgency.

4.Create a Distraction-Free Environment

Minimize distractions in your environment by eliminating clutter, turning off notifications, and creating physical barriers to external stimuli. Designate a specific workspace for focused work and establish boundaries to protect your concentration.

5. Practice Single-Tasking

Contrary to widespread belief, multitasking can diminish productivity and impair focus. Instead, focus on one task at a time, giving it your full attention before moving on to the next. Single tasking allows for deeper engagement and better-quality output.

6. Take Regular Breaks

Taking periodic breaks throughout the day helps prevent mental fatigue and maintain cognitive performance. Engage in activities that promote relaxation and rejuvenation, such as stretching, walking, or deep breathing exercises.

7. Exercise Regularly

Physical exercise has been shown to enhance cognitive function, including attention and focus. Incorporate regular exercise into your routine to boost energy levels, reduce stress, and improve overall brain health.

Conclusion

Improving focus is a skill that can be cultivated through deliberate practice and the adoption of effective techniques.

By incorporating mindfulness meditation, time management strategies, goal setting, and environmental modifications into your routine, you can enhance your ability to concentrate, increase productivity, and achieve greater success in all areas of life.

Experiment with different techniques to find the ones that work best for you and remember that consistent effort and patience are key to mastering the art of focus.

CHAPTER 4

Developing Concentration Skill.

Concentration is a skill that can be developed and honed over time. We discuss the importance of cultivating self-discipline and resilience in maintaining focus amidst challenges.

Focus is linked to productivity, as it enables us to efficiently allocate our time and energy to tasks that matter most. In this chapter, we discuss strategies for optimizing productivity through focus, such as prioritizing tasks, breaking them down into manageable chunks, and minimizing multitasking. We also explore techniques for maintaining focus during long work sessions and avoiding burnout.

Concentration, often referred to as the cornerstone of productivity and success, is a skill that can be cultivated and refined through deliberate practice and perseverance.

In this chapter, we will delve into various strategies and exercises aimed at enhancing concentration skills and unlocking your full cognitive potential.

1. Start with Mindfulness Meditation

Mindfulness meditation serves as an excellent foundation for developing concentration skills. Begin by dedicating a few minutes each day to mindfulness practice, focusing on your breath or bodily sensations. As you become more proficient, gradually increase the duration of your sessions.

2. Practice Deep Listening

Engage in deep listening exercises to sharpen your ability to sustain attention. Choose a piece of music or a natural sound, such as birdsong or rainfall and listen attentively without judgment or distraction.

Notice the nuances and subtleties of the sound, training your mind to remain focused and present.

3. Cultivate Single-Pointed Focus

Select a specific object or focal point, such as a candle flame or a geometric shape, and concentrate your gaze upon it. Whenever your mind begins to wander, gently redirect your attention back to the chosen point. This practice builds concentration by training the mind to remain fixed on a single target.

4. Practice Visualization Techniques

Imagery exercises involve visualizing vivid mental images with as much detail as possible. Close your eyes and imagine yourself in a serene, peaceful setting, such as a tranquil beach or a lush forest.

Engage all your senses to make the visualization as lifelike as possible, enhancing your ability to sustain focus and mental clarity.

5. Set Clear and Achievable Goals

Establish clear, achievable goals to provide direction and purpose for your concentration practice. Break down larger goals into smaller, actionable steps and set deadlines to create a sense of urgency. Tracking your progress and celebrating small victories along the way can further motivate you to stay focused and committed.

6.Create a Distraction-Free Environment

Designate a quiet, clutter-free space for concentration practice, free from distractions and interruptions. Silence your phone, close unnecessary tabs on your computer, and inform others of your need for uninterrupted focus.

Creating a conducive environment minimizes external distractions and maximizes your ability to concentrate.

7. Practice Regular Mindfulness Checks

Periodically check in with your mental state throughout the day, noting any signs of distraction or wandering attention. When you notice your mind drifting, gently bring it back to the present moment without judgment. Mindfulness checks help cultivate self-awareness and reinforce your commitment to maintaining focus.

8. Set Time Limits for Focus Sessions

Allocate dedicated time intervals for focused concentration, such as 25 or 30 minutes, followed by short breaks.

Use a timer to signal the start and end of each session and resist the temptation to deviate from your task during the allotted time.

Structured focus sessions promote discipline and consistency in your concentration practice.

9. Practice Patience and Persistence

Developing concentration skills is a gradual process that requires patience and persistence. Be kind to yourself and acknowledge that distractions and lapses in focus are natural occurrences. Approach each practice session with a sense of curiosity and openness, knowing that each moment of focused attention brings you one step closer to mastery.

Conclusion

Developing concentration skills is a journey of self-discovery and self-mastery that holds the promise of unlocking your full cognitive potential.

By incorporating mindfulness meditation, deep listening exercises, visualization techniques, and other strategies into your daily routine, you can cultivate a heightened sense of focus, clarity, and productivity.

Embrace the process with patience and persistence, knowing that the rewards of enhanced concentration extend far beyond the realm of productivity to encompass greater peace of mind and fulfillment in all aspects of life.

CHAPTER 5

Overcoming Common Focus Challenges

Even with the best intentions, maintaining focus can be challenging at times. In this chapter, we address common focus challenges and provide practical solutions for overcoming them. Whether it is dealing with procrastination, managing information overload, or navigating distractions in the digital age, we offer strategies to help readers stay on track and achieve their goals.

In the pursuit of productivity and excellence, it is not uncommon to encounter obstacles that hinder our ability to maintain focus. From distractions and procrastination to mental fatigue and lack of motivation, various challenges can impede our progress and derail our efforts. In this chapter, we will explore practical strategies for overcoming common focus problems and reclaiming control over our attention.

1. Procrastination Prevention

Procrastination can be a significant barrier to productivity, undermining our best intentions and delaying progress on important tasks. To overcome procrastination:

Break Tasks into Smaller Steps: Divide daunting tasks into smaller, more manageable components to reduce overwhelm and increase motivation to get started.

Set Clear Deadlines: Establish deadlines for tasks and hold yourself accountable for meeting them. Breaking tasks into smaller, time-bound chunks creates a sense of urgency and momentum.

Use the Two-Minute Rule: If a task can be completed in two minutes or less, do it immediately rather than deferring it. This small but powerful habit prevents tasks from accumulating and becoming overwhelming.

2. Mental Fatigue Management

Mental fatigue can sap our energy and impair cognitive function, making it challenging to maintain focus and productivity. To manage mental fatigue:

Take Regular Breaks: Schedule periodic breaks throughout the day to rest and recharge your mental faculties. Short breaks, even just a few minutes, can replenish cognitive resources and improve overall productivity.

Practice Mindfulness and Relaxation Techniques: Engage in mindfulness meditation, deep breathing exercises, or progressive muscle relaxation to reduce stress and promote mental clarity.

Prioritize Sleep and Recovery: Ensure you get an adequate amount of sleep each night and prioritize restorative activities such as exercise, leisure, and socializing to prevent burnout and maintain optimal cognitive function.

3. Lack of Motivation

Lack of motivation can stem from numerous factors, including boredom, fear of failure, or a lack of alignment with personal values. To boost motivation:

Set Meaningful Goals: Establish clear, compelling goals that align with your values and aspirations. Connecting tasks to larger objectives increases intrinsic motivation and enhances focus.

Celebrate Progress: Acknowledge and celebrate small victories along the way, recognizing the effort and dedication required to achieve them. Positive reinforcement reinforces motivation and sustains momentum.

Find Purpose and Passion: Cultivate a sense of purpose and passion in your work by identifying tasks that resonate with your interests, strengths, and values. Engaging in meaningful work fosters intrinsic motivation and fuels sustained focus.

Conclusion

By actively managing distractions, addressing and nurturing motivation, you can cultivate a focused and resilient mindset to achieve your goals with clarity and purpose.

Embrace challenges as opportunities for growth and leverage the strategies outlined in this chapter to navigate obstacles and unlock your full potential.

CHAPTER 6

Cultivating Focus in Everyday Life

In the hustle and bustle of modern life, cultivating focus is not just a luxury but a necessity for navigating the complexities of our daily routines with clarity and efficiency. In this chapter, we will explore practical strategies for infusing mindfulness and intentionality into everyday activities, fostering a culture of focus and presence in all aspects of life.

1. Mindful Morning Routine

Start your day with a mindful morning routine to set a positive tone for the day ahead. Begin by waking up at a consistent time and engaging in activities that promote a sense of calm and centeredness, such as meditation, stretching, or journaling. Approach each task mindfully, savoring the sensations and experiences as they unfold.

2. Intentional Task Management

Approach tasks with intentionality and purpose, rather than succumbing to autopilot or reactive modes of functioning. Before starting a task, take a moment to clarify your objectives and priorities, setting a clear intention for what you aim to accomplish. Break tasks into smaller, actionable steps and focus on completing them one at a time with full attention and presence.

3. Mindful Eating

Transform mealtime into an opportunity for mindfulness and sensory awareness. Slow down and savor each bite, paying attention to the flavors, textures, and sensations of the food. Practice mindful eating by chewing slowly, putting down utensils between bites, and cultivating gratitude for the nourishment and sustenance provided by the meal.

4. Digital Mindfulness

Mindfully engage with technology by setting boundaries and establishing mindful usage habits. Practice digital detoxes by taking regular breaks from screens and disconnecting from devices during designated periods of the day. Limit multitasking and practice single tasking, focusing on one digital task at a time with undivided attention.

5. Mindful Movement

Incorporate mindful movement practices, such as yoga, tai chi, or walking meditation, into your daily routine. Pay attention to the sensations of movement in your body, tuning into the rhythm of your breath and the sensations of muscle engagement and relaxation. Use movement as an opportunity to cultivate embodied presence and awareness.

6. Mindful Communication

Practice mindful communication in your interactions with others, whether in personal or professional contexts. Listen attentively, with an open heart and mind, to understand the perspectives and feelings of others. Pause before responding, allowing space for reflection and conscious choice of words. Cultivate empathy, compassion, and authenticity in your communication, fostering deeper connections and mutual understanding.

7. Evening Reflection

End your day with a period of evening reflection to review and integrate your experiences. Take stock of your accomplishments, challenges, and areas for growth, without judgment or self-criticism. Engage in relaxation practices, such as deep breathing or progressive muscle relaxation, to unwind and prepare for restful sleep.

Conclusion

Cultivating focus in everyday life is not a destination but a journey of continuous growth and self-discovery.

By infusing mindfulness and intentionality into daily activities, we can cultivate a culture of presence, purpose, and focus that enriches our lives and enhances our overall well-being.

Embrace each moment as an opportunity for mindful engagement and conscious living and watch as focus and clarity become guiding principles in your journey towards a more fulfilling and meaningful life.

CHAPTER 7

Harnessing Focus for Personal Growth

In this chapter, we will explore how harnessing focus can empower us to cultivate positive habits, overcome obstacles and realize our full potential. By focusing our attention on self-improvement goals, we can cultivate new skills, deepen our knowledge, and expand our horizons. We discuss the importance of setting clear objectives, developing a growth mindset, and embracing challenges as opportunities for learning and growth.

1. Clarify Your Vision

Focus begins with clarity of vision—a clear understanding of who you are, what you value, and where you want to go in life. Take time to reflect on your aspirations, passions, and goals, and distill them into a compelling vision for your future. Visualize your ideal self and the life you wish to create, anchoring your focus in a sense of purpose and direction.

2. Set SMART Goals

Transform your vision into actionable goals by setting Specific, Measurable, Achievable, Relevant, and Time-bound (SMART) objectives. Break down your long-term vision into smaller, manageable milestones, and prioritize them based on their significance and alignment with your values. Setting clear goals provides a roadmap for focus and guides your efforts towards meaningful progress.

3. Cultivate Self-Discipline

Self-discipline is the cornerstone of focus, enabling us to resist distractions, overcome procrastination, and stay committed to our goals. Cultivate self-discipline through consistent practice and habit formation, gradually strengthening your ability to prioritize tasks, manage time effectively, and stay on course despite challenges and temptations.

4. Embrace Growth Mindset

Adopt a growth mindset—a belief that our abilities and intelligence can be developed through dedication and effort—as a catalyst for personal growth and resilience. Cultivate a mindset of curiosity, resilience, and openness to learning, viewing challenges as opportunities for growth and setbacks as steppingstones towards success. Harness the power of focus to pursue continuous improvement and mastery in all areas of life.

5. Prioritize Self-Care

Nurture your physical, mental, and emotional well-being through regular self-care practices that replenish your energy and sustain your focus. Prioritize activities that promote relaxation, creativity, and connection, such as exercise, nature walks, hobbies, and spending time with loved ones. By caring for yourself holistically, you strengthen your capacity for focus and resilience, enabling you to thrive amidst life's challenges.

6. Reflect and Adapt

Regularly reflect on your progress and adjust your approach as needed to stay aligned with your goals and values. Celebrate your achievements and learn from setbacks, using each experience as an opportunity for self-reflection and growth. Embrace a spirit of adaptability and flexibility, remaining open to new opportunities and insights that emerge along your journey of personal growth.

Conclusion

Harnessing focus for personal growth requires intentionality, discipline, and self-awareness. By clarifying your vision, setting SMART goals, cultivating self-discipline, practicing mindfulness, embracing a growth mindset, prioritizing self-care, and reflecting on your journey, you can harness the transformative power of focus to cultivate positive habits, overcome obstacles and realize your full potential.

Embrace the journey of personal growth with courage and conviction, knowing that each moment of focused effort brings you one step closer to becoming the best version of yourself.

CHAPTER 8

The Role of Focus in Personal Relationships

In the intricate dance of personal relationships, focus serves as a guiding force, shaping the quality of connections and fostering intimacy, empathy, and mutual understanding.

In this chapter, we will explore the multifaceted role of focus in personal relationships and how cultivating attention can enrich our interactions and deepen our connections with others.

1. Presence and Engagement

Focus plays a pivotal role in fostering presence and engagement in personal relationships. When we are fully present with others, attentive to their words, emotions, and needs, we create a space for authentic connection and meaningful interaction.

By focusing our attention on the present moment and actively listening to others without distractions, we convey respect, empathy, and validation, nurturing trust, and intimacy in our relationships.

2. Active Listening

Active listening, a cornerstone of effective communication, relies on focused attention and genuine interest in understanding the perspectives and experiences of others.

By listening attentively, without interrupting or pre-judging, we signal our willingness to empathize and validate the feelings and concerns of our loved ones.

Active listening fosters deeper connections, promotes emotional intimacy and strengthens the bonds of trust and communication in personal relationships.

3. Emotional Intelligence

Focus enhances emotional intelligence—the ability to recognize, understand, and manage emotions in ourselves and others—in personal relationships.

By tuning into subtle emotional cues and nonverbal signals, we deepen our empathy and attunement to the feelings and needs of our partners, friends, and family members.

Cultivating emotional intelligence through focused attention enables us to navigate conflicts with grace, express empathy and compassion and cultivate greater harmony and mutual respect in our relationships.

4. Quality Time

Focus enables us to prioritize quality time with loved ones, carving out dedicated moments for connection, shared experiences, and meaningful conversations.

By setting aside distractions and devoting our full attention to the people we care about, we demonstrate our commitment to nurturing and sustaining our relationships. Whether it is sharing a meal, going for a walk, or engaging in a heartfelt conversation, quality time fosters closeness, strengthens bonds and reinforces the foundation of love and connection in personal relationships.

5. Building Trust and Intimacy

Focus is essential for building trust and intimacy in personal relationships, creating a safe and supportive environment where individuals can express themselves authentically and vulnerably.

When we focus our attention on our partners' needs, desires, and concerns, we demonstrate our investment in their well-being and the health of our relationship. By fostering open communication, active listening, and mutual respect, we cultivate trust, deepen intimacy, and foster a sense of security and belonging in our relationships.

Conclusion

In personal relationships, focus serves as a catalyst for connection, empathy, and intimacy, enriching our interactions and nurturing the bonds of love and friendship.

By cultivating presence, active listening, emotional intelligence, and quality time with loved ones, we strengthen the foundation of trust, respect and understanding that underpins healthy and fulfilling relationships.

Embrace the transformative power of focus in your personal connections and watch as your relationships flourish and thrive.

CHAPTER 9

Maintaining Focus in a Digital World

In an era defined by constant connectivity and digital distractions, maintaining focus has become a formidable challenge for many. However, with mindful strategies and intentional habits, it is possible to navigate the digital landscape with clarity and purpose. In this chapter, we will explore effective techniques for cultivating focus amidst the myriad temptations and disruptions of the digital world.

1. Set Clear Boundaries

Establish boundaries around your digital devices and online activities to minimize distractions and maintain focus. Designate specific times of day for checking emails, social media, and other digital notifications and resist the urge to engage with them outside of these designated windows. Create physical barriers, such as using website blockers or turning off notifications, to prevent interruptions during focused work or leisure time.

2. Practice Digital Detoxes

Regularly disconnect from digital devices and platforms to recharge your mental batteries and regain perspective. Schedule periods of digital detox, such as weekends or evenings, where you abstain from using smartphones, computers, and other screens. Use this time to engage in offline activities that nourish your mind, body, and spirit, such as spending time in nature, reading a book, or connecting with loved ones face-to-face.

3. Cultivate Digital Mindfulness

Practice digital mindfulness by bringing awareness and intentionality to your online interactions and usage habits. Before opening an app or website, pause for a moment to reflect on your intention and whether it aligns with your values and priorities. Set clear goals for your digital activities, such as seeking information, connecting with friends, or engaging in leisure and avoid mindless scrolling or browsing.

4. Implement Focus-Enhancing Tools

Utilize technological tools and apps designed to enhance focus and minimize distractions in the digital environment. Explore productivity apps that help you organize tasks, manage time effectively, and track progress towards goals.

Experiment with distraction-blocking tools, such as browser extensions or focus mode features, that limit access to distracting websites and social media platforms during focused work sessions.

5. Practice Single-Tasking

Embrace the power of single-tasking—focusing on one task at a time with undivided attention—instead of succumbing to the allure of multitasking. Prioritize important tasks and allocate dedicated time blocks for focused work, during which you commit to working on a single task without switching between activities.

By concentrating your efforts on one task at a time, you can increase productivity, enhance creativity and reduce mental fatigue.

6. Create a Distraction-Free Environment

Designate a distraction-free workspace where you can cultivate focus and concentration without interruptions. Minimize visual and auditory distractions by decluttering your physical environment, optimizing lighting and ergonomics, and using noise-canceling headphones if necessary.

Communicate your need for uninterrupted focus to colleagues, family members or roommates and establish clear boundaries to protect your concentration.

7. Foster Offline Connections

Nurture offline connections and experiences that foster presence, connection, and joy in the real world. Prioritize face-to-face interactions with friends, family, and community members, engaging in meaningful conversations and shared activities that nourish your soul. Spend time engaging in hobbies, pursuits, and experiences that bring you fulfillment and satisfaction beyond the digital realm.

Conclusion

Maintaining focus in a digital world requires intentional effort and mindful awareness of our digital habits and usage patterns. By setting clear boundaries, practicing digital detoxes, cultivating digital mindfulness, implementing focus-enhancing tools, practicing single-tasking, creating a distraction-free environment, and fostering offline connections, we can reclaim our attention and cultivate deeper focus amidst the distractions of the digital age. Embrace these strategies with intentionality and consistency and watch as your ability to focus and thrive in the digital world blossoms.

CHAPTER 10

Cultivating Focus in the Workplace

Focus is a critical asset in the professional realm, where productivity and performance are paramount. In this chapter, we examine how cultivating focus can enhance workplace efficiency, creativity, and collaboration. We discuss strategies for minimizing workplace distractions, optimizing task prioritization, and fostering a culture of focused work. Additionally, we explore the role of leadership in creating environments that support employee focus and well-being, contributing to organizational success and growth.

1. Establish Clear Goals and Priorities

Clarity of purpose is essential for cultivating focus in the workplace. Ensure that employees understand the organization's mission, vision, and strategic objectives, and align their individual goals and tasks accordingly. Set clear expectations and priorities for projects, tasks, and deadlines, empowering employees to focus their efforts on the most important and impactful work.

2 Provide Distraction-Free Environment

Create a workspace that minimizes distractions and supports focused work. Designate quiet zones or dedicated areas for focused tasks, equipped with ergonomic furniture and adequate lighting.

Encourage employees to use tools and technologies that minimize interruptions, such as noise-canceling headphones or distraction-blocking apps and establish norms around communication and collaboration to reduce unnecessary interruptions.

3. Encourage Time Management and Prioritization

Empower employees to manage their time effectively and prioritize tasks based on importance and urgency. Provide training and resources on time management techniques, such as the Eisenhower Matrix or Pomodoro Technique, to help employees organize their workload and allocate time for focused work.

Encourage regular reviews of priorities and progress to ensure alignment with organizational goals and objectives.

4. Foster a Culture of Deep Work

Promote a culture of deep work—a state of focused and undisturbed concentration on cognitively demanding tasks—in the workplace.

Encourage employees to schedule dedicated blocks of time for deep work, free from distractions and interruptions. Provide support and recognition for employees who demonstrate mastery in their craft and deliver high-quality work through sustained focus and concentration.

5. Model and Reinforce Focus

Lead by example by demonstrating focused behavior and prioritizing deep work in your own work habits. Avoid multitasking and minimize distractions during meetings and collaborative sessions to create an environment conducive to focused thinking and decision-making. Recognize and celebrate instances of focused effort and achievement, reinforcing the value of concentration and attention to detail in driving organizational success.

6. Provide Opportunities for Skill Development

Invest in training and development programs that equip employees with the skills and strategies needed to enhance focus and concentration. Offer workshops on mindfulness, attention management and cognitive fitness to help employees strengthen their ability to maintain focus amidst distractions. Provide resources and support for employees to develop healthy habits, such as regular exercise, adequate sleep, and stress management techniques, that promote cognitive function and focus.

7. Foster a Supportive and Collaborative Culture

Create a supportive and collaborative work environment where employees feel valued, respected, and empowered to contribute their best work. Encourage open communication and feedback, fostering a culture of trust and psychological safety that enables employees to express their ideas and concerns without fear of judgment or retribution. Foster opportunities for social connection and camaraderie, recognizing the importance of balanced work-life integration in sustaining focus and well-being.

Conclusion

Cultivating focus in the workplace is a collective endeavor that requires alignment of organizational practices, individual behaviors, and cultural norms.

By establishing clear goals, providing a distraction-free environment, encouraging time management and prioritization, fostering a culture of deep work, modeling and reinforcing focus, providing opportunities for skill development, and fostering a supportive and collaborative culture, organizations can empower employees to thrive in their roles and achieve their highest potential.

Embrace these strategies with intentionality and commitment and watch as focus becomes a driving force for innovation, productivity and success in the workplace.

CHAPTER 11

The Connection Between Focus and Well-being

Focus is not just about achieving external goals; it also plays a fundamental role in our overall well-being and quality of life. In this chapter, we explore the connection between focus and well-being, highlighting the importance of mental clarity, emotional balance, and inner peace. We discuss mindfulness practices, stress reduction techniques, and self-care strategies that promote focus and holistic well-being. By prioritizing self-care and nurturing our mental and emotional health, we can cultivate a sense of balance and fulfillment that enhances our capacity for focus and resilience.

In the pursuit of well-being, focus serves as both a catalyst and a cornerstone, influencing our mental, emotional and physical health in profound ways. In this chapter, we'll explore the intricate relationship between focus and well-being and how cultivating attention can enhance our overall quality of life.

1. Mental Well-being

Focus plays a pivotal role in promoting mental well-being by reducing stress, anxiety and rumination. When we're able to direct our attention towards the present moment, we cultivate a sense of calm and clarity that mitigates the negative impact of intrusive thoughts and worries.

Mindfulness practices, such as meditation and deep breathing, strengthen our ability to regulate emotions and maintain perspective, fostering resilience and emotional balance.

2. Emotional Well-being

Emotional well-being is closely intertwined with our ability to focus and regulate our attention. By cultivating emotional intelligence and attunement through focused awareness, we deepen our understanding of our own emotions and those of others, fostering empathy, compassion, and authentic connections. Focused attention enables us to respond thoughtfully to challenging situations, rather than reacting impulsively out of fear or anger, thereby promoting healthier relationships and greater emotional resilience.

3. Physical Well-being

The connection between focus and physical well-being is evident in the impact of stress and distractions on our body's systems. Chronic stress and cognitive overload can manifest as physical symptoms such as tension headaches, muscle pain and gastrointestinal discomfort.

By reducing stress and enhancing focus through mindfulness practices and stress management techniques, we promote optimal functioning of the body's immune, digestive and cardiovascular systems, supporting overall health and well-being.

4. Cognitive Well-being

Cognitive well-being encompasses our cognitive functioning and mental agility, which are influenced by our ability to focus and sustain attention. By engaging in activities that challenge and stimulate the mind, such as problem-solving, learning new skills and creative pursuits, we promote neuroplasticity and cognitive resilience. Focused attention enhances memory consolidation, information processing and decision-making, optimizing cognitive function and promoting lifelong learning and intellectual growth.

5. Social Well-being

Focus is essential for fostering meaningful connections and nurturing supportive relationships, which are fundamental to our social well-being. When we're fully present and attentive in our interactions with others, we create space for genuine connection and mutual understanding. By listening actively, empathizing with others' experiences and communicating authentically, we strengthen the bonds of trust and intimacy that enrich our social connections and contribute to our overall sense of belonging and fulfill me.

Conclusion

The connection between focus and well-being underscores the profound impact of attention on our mental, emotional and physical health.

By cultivating focused awareness and attentional control through mindfulness practices, stress management techniques, and healthy lifestyle habits, we empower ourselves to nurture well-being in all aspects of our lives.

Embrace the transformative power of focus as a pathway to greater resilience, fulfillment, and flourishing and watch as your well-being thrives amidst the beauty of mindful presence and intentional living.

CHAPTER 12

Mastering Focus for a Fulfilling Life

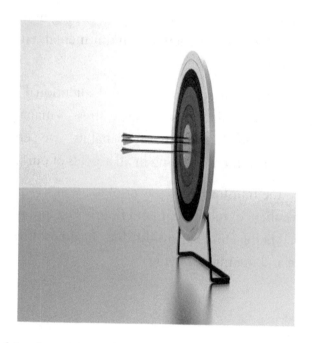

In this chapter, we bring together the key insights and strategies discussed so far to empower readers to master focus and create a fulfilling life.

We emphasize the importance of intentionality, perseverance and self-awareness in cultivating focus as a lifelong skill.

By integrating focus into all aspects of our lives—personal, professional, and relational—we can unlock our full potential, pursue our passions with purpose and experience greater joy, meaning and fulfillment.

Remember, the journey to mastering focus is not always easy, but it is immensely rewarding, leading to a life lived with intention, clarity, and impact.

1. Clarify Your Values and Priorities

Mastering focus begins with clarity of purpose and alignment with our values and priorities. Take time to reflect on what matters most to you in life—your passions, aspirations and core values. Define your long-term vision for a fulfilling life and identify the actions and choices that will bring you closer to realizing that vision. By aligning your focus with your values and priorities, you lay the foundation for a life of purpose and meaning.

2. Cultivate Presence and Mindfulness

Presence and mindfulness are essential ingredients for mastering focus and living fully in the present moment. Cultivate practices such as meditation, deep breathing and sensory awareness to anchor yourself in the here and now. Embrace each moment with curiosity and openness, savoring the richness of experience and finding beauty in the ordinary. By cultivating presence and mindfulness, you deepen your connection to yourself, others and the world around you, enriching your life with depth and authenticity.

3. Embrace the Power of Choice

Focus empowers us to make conscious choices that align with our values and aspirations. Recognize that you have the power to choose how you direct your attention and energy in each moment. Let go of distractions and obligations that do not serve your greater purpose, and instead, invest your focus in activities and relationships that bring you joy, fulfillment, and growth. By embracing the power of choice, you reclaim agency over your life and create space for what truly matters to you.

4. Practice Gratitude and Appreciation

Gratitude is a potent antidote to distraction and discontent, anchoring us in the present moment and fostering a sense of abundance and appreciation for life's blessings.

Cultivate a daily practice of gratitude, reflecting on the things, experiences, and relationships that enrich your life. By shifting your focus towards gratitude and appreciation, you cultivate a positive mindset and cultivate resilience in the face of challenges, paving the way for a more fulfilling and meaningful life.

5. Pursue Flow and Engagement

Flow, a state of deep absorption and effortless concentration, is a hallmark of a fulfilling life. Seek out activities and pursuits that immerse you fully in the present moment, challenging your skills and stretching your abilities.

Whether it's pursuing a passion project, engaging in creative expression, or immersing yourself in nature, prioritize activities that evoke a sense of flow and engagement.

By cultivating moments of flow in your daily life, you tap into a source of intrinsic motivation and fulfillment that transcends external rewards.

Conclusion

Mastering focus is not just about sharpening your attention; it's about unlocking the door to a life of purpose, presence, and fulfillment.

By clarifying your values and priorities, cultivating presence and mindfulness, embracing the power of choice, practicing gratitude and appreciation, and pursuing flow and engagement, you harness the transformative power of focus to create a life that resonates with meaning and joy.

Embrace each moment as an opportunity for growth and self-discovery and let the journey of mastering focus lead you towards a life of profound fulfillment and flourishing.

CHAPTER 13

Nurturing Focus in Learning and Education

Focus is fundamental to effective learning and academic success. In this chapter, we explore how students can cultivate focus to enhance their learning experience and academic performance.

We discuss strategies for improving concentration during study sessions, managing distractions in the classroom, and staying engaged in learning activities.

Additionally, we examine the role of educators in creating environments that support student focus, fostering a culture of curiosity and active participation, and providing tools and resources to help students develop their focus skills.

1. Create a Supportive Learning Environment

Establish a supportive and conducive learning environment that minimizes distractions and promotes focused engagement. Design classrooms with comfortable seating, adequate lighting, and minimal visual clutter to optimize concentration. Encourage students to turn off digital devices or use them exclusively for educational purposes during class time, fostering an atmosphere of attentiveness and respect for learning.

2. Set Clear Learning Objectives

Communicate clear learning objectives and expectations to students, providing a roadmap for focused study and academic achievement. Break down complex concepts into manageable units and outline the skills and knowledge students are expected to acquire. By providing clear guidance and direction, you empower students to channel their focus towards specific learning goals, enhancing their motivation and sense of purpose.

3. Foster Active Learning Techniques

Promote active learning techniques that engage students' minds and bodies in the learning process, fostering deeper understanding and retention of course material.

Encourage interactive discussions, collaborative projects, and hands-on activities that require active participation and critical thinking.

By actively engaging with course content, students develop their ability to sustain attention and deepen their understanding of complex concepts.

4. Teach Mindfulness and Attention Management

Integrate mindfulness and attention management practices into the curriculum to help students cultivate focused awareness and concentration skills. Teach techniques such as mindful breathing, meditation, and sensory awareness to help students develop the capacity to regulate their attention and stay present in the moment. By nurturing mindfulness skills, you equip students with valuable tools for navigating distractions and optimizing their learning potential.

5. Provide Regular Feedback and Support

Offer timely feedback and support to students to help them stay on track and make progress towards their learning goals. Provide constructive feedback on assignments, assessments, and class participation, highlighting areas of strength and opportunities for growth. Offer additional resources, tutoring, or academic support services to students who may need extra assistance in maintaining focus or mastering challenging concepts.

6. Encourage Breaks and Movement

Recognize the importance of breaks and movement in sustaining focus and cognitive performance.

Encourage students to take regular breaks during study sessions or class lectures to rest and recharge their mental energy. Incorporate movement breaks, such as stretching or short walks, into the classroom routine to promote circulation and alleviate physical tension.

By encouraging breaks and movement, you support students' overall well-being and enhance their ability to maintain focus over extended periods.

7. Foster a Growth Mindset

Cultivate a growth mindset culture that emphasizes the value of effort, perseverance, and resilience in the learning process.

Encourage students to view challenges as opportunities for growth and learning, rather than obstacles to success.

Provide praise and recognition for students' efforts and progress, reinforcing the belief that intelligence and abilities can be developed through dedication and practice.

By fostering a growth mindset, you empower students to embrace challenges with confidence and maintain focus in pursuit of their academic goals.

Conclusion

Nurturing focus in learning and education is essential for empowering students to thrive academically and develop the skills they need for success in school and beyond.

By creating a supportive learning environment, setting clear objectives, fostering active learning techniques, teaching mindfulness and attention management,

providing regular feedback and support, encouraging breaks and movement, and fostering a growth mindset, educators can help students cultivate the focused

attention and engagement necessary for lifelong learning and intellectual growth.

Embrace these strategies with intentionality and compassion and watch as students unlock their full potential and embark on a journey of discovery and self-improvement.

CHAPTER 14

Fostering Focus in Creative Pursuits

Creativity flourishes in an environment of focused attention and immersion. In this chapter, we explore how artists, writers, musicians, and other creatives can cultivate focus to enhance their creative process and productivity. We discuss techniques for overcoming creative blocks, maintaining flow states, and harnessing focused attention to bring creative visions to life. Additionally, we examine the importance of balance between focused work and periods of rest and relaxation to replenish creative energy and prevent burnout.

1. Create a Dedicated Creative Space

Establish a dedicated space for creative work that is free from distractions and conducive to focused engagement. Designate a room, corner, or workspace where you can immerse yourself fully in your creative pursuits without interruption. Personalize your creative space with inspiring decor, artwork, and tools that spark your imagination and ignite your creativity.

2. Set Clear Intentions and Goals

Clarify your intentions and goals for your creative endeavors, outlining the outcomes you hope to achieve and the milestones you aim to reach along the way. Set specific, measurable, and achievable goals that provide direction and focus for your creative work. By defining clear objectives, you create a roadmap for focused action and progress in your creative pursuits.

3. Embrace Constraints as Catalysts for Creativity

View constraints as opportunities rather than limitations in your creative process. Embrace constraints such as time limits, budget constraints, or technical limitations as catalysts for innovation and creative problem-solving.

Constraints force you to think creatively, experiment with new approaches, and push the boundaries of what is possible, fostering resilience and adaptability in your creative practice.

4. Cultivate Deep Work and Flow States

Cultivate deep work and flow states—states of immersive focus and heightened concentration—in your creative process.

Set aside dedicated blocks of time for focused creative work, free from distractions and interruptions.

Engage in activities that promote flow, such as sketching, writing, or composing music, where you lose track of time and become fully absorbed in the creative process. By cultivating deep focus and flow, you tap into a reservoir of creative energy and inspiration that fuels your artistic expression.

5. Practice Mindful Creativity

Infuse mindfulness into your creative practice by bringing focused awareness and intentionality to each stage of the creative process. Practice mindfulness techniques such as deep breathing, meditation, or mindful observation to quiet the mind, enhance concentration, and tap into your creative intuition.

Cultivate a beginner's mind—a sense of curiosity, openness, and non-judgment—in your creative exploration, allowing new ideas and insights to emerge organically.

6. Embrace Solitude and Reflection

Create space for solitude and reflection in your creative practice, allowing yourself time to recharge, rejuvenate, and reconnect with your creative vision.

Schedule regular periods of quiet reflection, away from distractions and external stimuli, to contemplate ideas, brainstorm solutions, and envision new possibilities. Solitude provides a fertile ground for creativity to flourish, allowing you to delve deep into your imagination and uncover hidden insights and inspirations.

7. Foster a Supportive Creative Community

Surround yourself with a supportive creative community that inspires, encourages, and challenges you to grow as an artist. Seek out like-minded individuals who share your passion for creativity and are committed to nurturing their craft.

Collaborate with fellow artists, participate in workshops or critique groups, and engage in constructive dialogue and feedback that enriches your creative practice. By fostering a supportive creative community, you create a nurturing environment where creativity can thrive and flourish.

Conclusion

Fostering focus in creative pursuits is essential for unlocking your creative potential and bringing your artistic visions to life.

By creating a dedicated creative space, setting clear intentions and goals, embracing constraints, cultivating deep work and flow states, practicing mindful creativity, embracing solitude and reflection, and fostering a supportive creative community, you empower yourself to cultivate focused attention and unleash your creativity in its fullest expression.

Embrace these strategies with passion and dedication and watch as your creative pursuits become a source of joy, fulfillment, and artistic mastery.

CHAPTER 15

The power of Focus in Sports and Performance

Focus is a critical factor in athletic performance and success in competitive sports. In this chapter, we explore how athletes can cultivate mental focus to optimize their physical performance and achieve peak results. We discuss techniques for developing pre-performance routines, managing performance anxiety, and maintaining focus under pressure. Additionally, we examine the role of visualization, self-talk, and mindfulness in enhancing athletic focus and confidence, enabling athletes to perform at their best when it matters most.

1. Enhancing Concentration and Attention

Focus is the foundation of peak performance in sports, enabling athletes to direct their attention with precision and clarity amidst the chaos of competition. By honing concentration skills through focused attention training, athletes sharpen their ability to block out distractions, maintain situational awareness, and execute with precision under pressure.

2. Channeling Mental Energy and Resilience

Focus serves as a conduit for channeling mental energy and resilience in sports, allowing athletes to harness their inner resources and overcome adversity with grace and determination. Through focused visualization, goal-setting, and positive self-talk, athletes cultivate mental toughness and resilience that fortify their resolve in the face of challenges and setbacks.

3. Maximizing Performance and Skill Mastery

Focus is the linchpin of skill mastery and performance optimization in sports, enabling athletes to refine their technique, strategy, and execution with meticulous attention to detail. By immersing themselves fully in the present moment and committing to deliberate practice, athletes accelerate their learning curve, refine their motor skills, and achieve peak performance levels that transcend their previous limitations.

4. Managing Pressure and Stress

Focus empowers athletes to manage pressure and stress with composure and confidence, transforming adversity into opportunity and doubt into determination. Through focused breathing, centering techniques, and mental rehearsal, athletes cultivate a state of relaxed alertness that enables them to perform at their best when the stakes are highest.

5. Cultivating Flow States and Peak Experiences

Focus unlocks the doorway to flow states—states of optimal performance and peak experience—in sports, where athletes experience a seamless fusion of action and awareness, effortlessness, and enjoyment. By cultivating focused attention, athletes enter a state of flow where time seems to stand still, and their performance transcends the ordinary, reaching heights of excellence and mastery previously thought impossible.

6. Building Team Cohesion and Collective Focus

Focus is not just an individual endeavor but a collective force that binds teams together and propels them towards shared goals and victories. By fostering a culture of focus and accountability within the team, athletes cultivate a sense of unity, purpose, and trust that amplifies their collective performance and resilience in the face of adversity.

7. Embracing the Journey of Mastery

Focus is not just a means to an end but a lifelong journey of mastery and self-discovery in sports.

By embracing the process of continuous improvement, athletes cultivate a growth mindset that fuels their passion for excellence and fuels their drive to push beyond their limits.

With each focused effort and intentional practice session, athletes' inch closer to realizing their full potential and leaving a legacy of greatness in their sport.

Conclusion

The power of focus in sports and performance is undeniable—a force that propels athletes towards greatness, resilience, and peak achievement.

By harnessing the transformative power of focus to enhance concentration and attention, channel mental energy and resilience, maximize performance and skill mastery, manage pressure and stress, cultivate flow states and peak experiences, build team cohesion and collective focus.

By embracing the journey of mastery, athletes unlock their full potential and redefine the boundaries of human achievement.

Embrace the power of focus with passion and determination and watch as your performance soars to new heights of excellence and fulfillment in sports and beyond.

CHAPTER 16

Harnessing Focus for Personal Projects and Goals

Whether pursuing personal projects or striving to achieve long-term goals, focus is essential for staying on track and making progress. In this chapter, we explore how individuals can harness focus to turn their dreams and aspirations into reality.

We discuss strategies for setting clear goals, creating action plans, and maintaining motivation and discipline throughout the journey.

Additionally, we examine the role of accountability partners, support networks, and regular self-reflection in sustaining focus and momentum toward achieving personal success and fulfillment.

In the realm of personal projects and goals, focus is the guiding force that transforms dreams into reality and aspirations into achievements.

In this chapter, we'll explore how harnessing focus can empower individuals to pursue their passions, achieve their goals, and create meaningful change in their lives.

1. Define Your Vision and Objectives

Start by clarifying your vision and defining clear objectives for your personal projects and goals.

What do you hope to accomplish? What is your ultimate vision for success? By articulating your goals with specificity and intentionality, you create a roadmap for focused action and progress.

2. Break Down Goals into Manageable Tasks

Break down your goals into manageable tasks and action steps that you can tackle one at a time. Focus on small, achievable milestones that build momentum and create a sense of progress. By breaking your goals into bite-sized chunks, you prevent overwhelm and make it easier to maintain focus on the task at hand.

3. Prioritize and Eliminate Distractions

Identify potential distractions and obstacles that may derail your focus and take proactive steps to mitigate them. Prioritize your tasks based on their importance and urgency and allocate dedicated time blocks for focused work. Create a distraction-free environment by minimizing interruptions and setting boundaries around your time and attention.

4. Set Clear Boundaries and Limits

Establish clear boundaries and limits around your personal projects and goals to protect your focus and energy. Learn to say no to commitments and distractions that don't align with your priorities. Set boundaries around your time and availability and communicate them assertively to others. By protecting your focus, you create space for deep work and meaningful progress.

5. Cultivate a Growth Mindset

Embrace a growth mindset—a belief in your ability to learn and grow through effort and persistence—as you pursue your personal projects and goals. View challenges and setbacks as opportunities for learning and growth, rather than obstacles to success. By adopting a growth mindset, you cultivate resilience and perseverance in the face of adversity, fueling your commitment to your goals.

6. Practice Time Management and Self-Discipline

Develop strong time management and self-discipline habits to optimize your focus and productivity. Use tools and techniques such as time blocking, to-do lists, and prioritization to organize your tasks and maximize your efficiency. Cultivate self-discipline by setting clear routines and sticking to them, even when faced with distractions or temptation.

7. Celebrate Progress and Milestones

Celebrate your progress and milestones along the way as you work towards your personal projects and goals. Take time to acknowledge your achievements and recognize the effort and dedication you've invested. Celebrating small wins boosts morale, reinforces positive habits, and motivates you to keep moving forward.

Conclusion

Harnessing focus for personal projects and goals is a transformative journey that empowers individuals to pursue their passions, achieve their dreams, and create meaningful change in their lives.

By defining your vision and objectives, breaking down goals into manageable tasks, prioritizing and eliminating distractions, setting clear boundaries and limits, cultivating a growth mindset, practicing time management and self-discipline, and celebrating progress and milestones, you unlock the full potential of your focus to drive meaningful progress and fulfillment in your personal endeavors.

Embrace the power of focus with intentionality and determination and watch as your dreams become reality before your eyes.

CHAPTER 17

Cultivating Focus in Spiritual Practice

Focus plays a central role in spiritual practice, enabling individuals to deepen their connection with themselves and the divine. In this chapter, we explore how mindfulness, meditation, and contemplative practices can cultivate spiritual focus and awareness. We discuss techniques for quieting the mind, cultivating inner stillness, and fostering a sense of presence and

Additionally, we examine the role of community and sacred rituals in supporting spiritual focus and fostering a sense of belonging and interconnectedness with all beings. Cultivating focus in spiritual practice is essential for deepening your connection with your chosen path and enhancing your overall well-being. Here are some strategies to help you develop and maintain focus in your spiritual journey:

1.Set Clear Intentions:

Begin each session with a clear intention or goal. Whether it's cultivating compassion, finding inner peace, or deepening your understanding, having a specific purpose can help direct your focus.

2.Create a Sacred Space:

Designate a quiet and comfortable space for your spiritual practice. Make it a place where you feel relaxed and free from distractions. You can adorn it with meaningful objects such as candles, crystals.

3.Establish a Routine:

Consistency is key to developing focus. Establish a regular practice schedule that works for you, whether it's daily meditation, weekly rituals, or monthly retreats. Over time, this routine will help train your mind to settle into the practice more easily.

4. Practice Mindfulness:

Incorporate mindfulness techniques into your spiritual practice cultivating present-moment awareness. Pay attention to your breath, bodily sensations, and thoughts without judgment. This can help quiet the mind and deepen your connection to the present! moment.

5.Use Rituals and Ceremonies:

Rituals and ceremonies can serve as powerful anchors for focus and intention. Whether it's lighting a candle, chanting a mantra, or performing a sacred dance, engaging in rituals can help you enter a state of heightened awareness and concentration.

6.Utilize Meditation Techniques:

Explore different meditation techniques such as concentration meditation (focusing on a single point of attention), mindfulness meditation (observing thoughts and sensations without attachment), or loving-kindness meditation (cultivating feelings of compassion and goodwill). Find the techniques that resonate with you and incorporate them into your practice.

7.Limit Distractions:

Minimize external distractions during your spiritual practice by turning off electronic devices, closing the door, or using earplugs if necessary. Create boundaries to protect your practice time and ensure. that you can fully immerse yourself in the experience.

8.Stay Grounded:

Stay grounded in your body and connected to the Earth during your spiritual practice. You can do this through grounding exercises such as walking barefoot in nature, gardening, or simply visualizing roots extending from your body into the earth.

9.Practice Self-Compassion:

Be patient and compassionate with yourself as you cultivate focus in your spiritual practice. It's natural for the mind to wander, and you may encounter obstacles along the way. Instead of judging yourself, gently guide your attention back to your chosen focal point with kindness and understanding.

10.Seek Guidance and Support

Don't hesitate to seek guidance from spiritual! teachers, mentors, or community members who can offer support and encouragement on your journey.

Sharing experiences and insights with others can enrich your practice and help you stay motivated.

By incorporating these strategies into your spiritual practice, you can cultivate greater focus, clarity, and presence, leading to deeper insights and spiritual growth.

Is this conversation helpful so far?

CHAPTER 18

Conclusion: Embracing Focus as a Way of Life

In this final chapter, we reflect on the transformative power of focus and its profound impact on every aspect of our lives. We emphasize the importance of embracing focus as a way of life—a guiding principle that informs our thoughts, actions, and relationships. By prioritizing focus, we can unlock our full potential, cultivate meaningful connections, and live with purpose, passion, and presence.

Embracing focus as a way of life extends beyond specific spiritual practices and encompasses all aspects of your daily routine and mindset. Here are some ways to integrate focus into your life:

1.Set Clear Goals:

Define your short-term and long-term goals across different areas of your life, such as career, relationships, health, and personal growth. Having clear objectives provide a sense of direction and purpose, allowing you to channel your energy and attention toward meaningful pursuits.

2.Prioritize Tasks:

Identify the most important tasks and priorities each! day and focus your efforts on completing them before moving on to less critical activities. This helps prevent. overwhelm and ensures that you make progress! toward your goals consistently.

3.Practice Single-Tasking:

Rather than trying to juggle multiple tasks simultaneously, focus on one task at a time and give it your full attention. This approach not only enhances productivity but also allows you to engage more deeply with each activity, leading to better outcomes and a greater sense of satisfaction.

4.Minimize Distractions:

Take proactive steps to minimize distractions in your environment, whether it's turning off notifications on your phone, creating a clutter-free workspace, or setting boundaries with people who may interrupt your focus. Cultivating a conducive environment supports your ability to maintain concentration and flow.

5.Cultivate Mindfulness:

Integrate mindfulness into your daily life by bringing awareness to the present moment in all that you do. Whether you're eating, walking, or having a conversation, practice being fully present and attentive without judgment.

Mindfulness enhances focus, reduces stress, and fosters a deeper appreciation for life's experiences.

6.Manage Time Wisely:

Use time management techniques such as the Pomodoro Technique, time blocking, or creating to-do. lists to structure your day effectively and allocate time. for tasks based on their importance and urgency. By managing your time wisely, you can optimize. productivity and create space for rest and relaxation.

7.Practice Self-Discipline:

- Cultivate self-discipline by honoring your commitments, following through on your goals, and staying accountable to yourself. This may involve making sacrifices in the short term to achieve long-term success and fulfillment. Strengthening your self-discipline muscle enhances your ability to stay focused despite challenges and distractions.

8.Embrace Deep Work:

- Embrace the concept of deep work, which involves dedicating uninterrupted blocks of time to focus on cognitively demanding tasks that require concentration and creativity. By immersing yourself fully in deep work sessions, you can achieve higher levels of productivity and produce high-quality work.

9.Reflect Regularly:

- Take time to reflect on your progress, achievements, and areas for growth regularly.

- Self-reflection allows you to course-correct, refine your goals, and cultivate a deeper understanding of yourself and your priorities. It also reinforces your commitment to living with intention and focus.

- Practice Patience and Persistence: Embracing focus as a way of life is a journey that requires patience, persistence, and self-compassion.

- Be gentle with yourself as you navigate challenges and setbacks and celebrate your progress along the way. Remember that each moment is an opportunity to recommit to your path and deepen your practice of focus.

Mastering focus is a lifelong journey that requires dedication, practice, and continuous refinement.

By understanding the principles of focus, identifying factors that affect our concentration, and implementing proven techniques and strategies, we can unlock our full potential and achieve greater success in all areas of our lives.

Remember, the ability to focus is not just a skill—it's a superpower that empowers us to shape our reality and create the life we desire.

Let this booklet serve as a roadmap on your journey to mastering focus and unleashing your full potential. Let us embark on this journey of self-discovery and growth, knowing that with focus as our compass, we can navigate life's challenges and opportunities with clarity, courage, and grace.

Made in the USA
Las Vegas, NV
10 July 2024

92131071R00056